COWBOYS, COWGIRLS & WIDE OPEN SPACES

by Jon Sheppard
Foreword by Barry Corbin

Published by:
Jon Sheppard Publishing

Designed by:
Keri Stevens
350 Third Avenue #317, New York, NY 10010. 212.741.1610
6300 N. Sage Wood Dr. #H315, Park City, UT 84098. 435.655.3990

If there are errors in names, places, or things the author apologizes.

Jon Sheppard
P.O. Box 18101, Avon, CO. 81620
jonshepp@vail.net
www.JonSheppardPhotography.com

10 9 8 7 63 5 4 3 2 1

Library of Congress Catalog Card Number 2001118971

Sheppard, J. 1942

Cowboys, Cowgirls & Wide Open Spaces

Photography

1. Non-fiction - Authorship, 1.Title II
Title: Cowboys, Cowgirls & Wide Open Spaces

0-9658009-2-X

Printed in Hong Kong through **Bolton Associates**,
San Rafael, CA.

ACKNOWLEDGEMENTS

Over the years I have traveled and met many wonderful people. In fact, I don't remember the names of many. I just know they helped me along the way. I like to thank the ranchers and cowboys who have made me feel so welcomed and appreciated. They too, are a special group of people. Black Mountain Ranch in Colorado, the Padlock Ranch in Wyoming, the Bell Ranch in New Mexico, the Coyote Moon Ranch in Colorado, the Mancos Valley Stage Line in Mancos, Colorado, Bernie and Suanne Holtman of the Texas Cowboys' Christmas Ball, Marsha Gustafson and the lovely people at the National Ranching Heritage Center in Lubbock, Texas, Staten Creek Ranch, Texas, all get my thanks. I know I have missed some names along the way, but they are still dear to my heart.

On the production side of things a great help from Bruce Chatterton and Peggy Sundberg for editing my work. Bob Singh of Singh-Ray filters for his wonderful filters that sharpen and add extra zip to my images. Good ol' Al Ansted for his technical comments on equipment and composure. A special "thank you" to Barry Corbin for his kindness in doing the foreword.
And most of all to He that has given me eternal life.

**This is dedicated to all the cowboy and cowgirls,
young and old alike, who have ever lived and traveled the trails,
and wide open spaces...if only in their dreams.**

©2001 BARRY CORBIN / ARMANDO TAMEZ

FOREWORD

My name is Barry Corbin. I make my living as an actor. My avocation is raising horses, dogs, and Texas Longhorn cattle. I've ridden the range all over the Great American West both on the screen and in reality. One of the fringe benefits of my business is meeting people in all walks of life and in all circumstances. I can't go as far as Will Rogers in saying "I never met a man I didn't like," but I can say I've liked most of 'em. The people I feel the most affinity for are people who deal on some level with cattle and horses. They're my kind of folks. I've helped friends gather, brand, and doctor cattle all the way from the Mexican border to Alberta, Canada, and from California to Eastern Oklahoma. I can say without equivocation the Cow People are the "Salt of the Earth." They have their different styles, of course. You can always tell a Nevada Buckaroo from a south Texas Vaquero, but they all have one thing in common, a deep and abiding love and sense of stewardship for the land...Their land...The West.

In this time of uncertainty for our Land, I think it's important to take a few minutes to look at what we have and what is, if necessary, worth fighting for. Jon Sheppard's photographic essays are one good way to do this. I am very impressed with his work. He captures in his pictures things that most of us never have the opportunity to see. Whether you live in New York or on the beach in California, viewing Jon's beautiful photographs and reading his inspiring prose will show you an America where hard work, sacrifice, and just plain having fun is still in vogue.

Barry Corbin
Ft. Worth, Texas

PREFACE

Throughout my travels all over the West I have enjoyed photographing the scenic beauty that makes this country so wonderful. The first time I saw the tall, majestic, snow-capped Rocky Mountains I was mesmerized. The rivers and streams that tumble out of the high country gurgle and splash with magic. They carry life-giving water to the lands far away. Across the ever expanding plains the sun seems to hang forever. The warm, gentle winds whistle through wheat fields and prairie grasses. Late in the afternoon the blackening of the summer sky ushers in lightening, thunder and much needed rain. When winter comes screaming in you may discover what a blizzard is. Snow builds up wherever it finds a place to stop. But the winter snows bring water for the summer crops and communities. In the deep, wide fertile valleys, or out on the wide open spaces you will find small towns, ghost towns, farms and ranches. Scattered along the way they bring an element of romance from the frontier days of old.

This is where the story begins. When I'm out on the highways and byways and see cattle feeding or horses grazing. Sometimes there are mountains behind them, or maybe majestic rolling plains, but there is always the deep blue western sky. In the afternoon light I may catch a herd of horses running through a field kicking up dust as they go. There is a farmer tilling the soil or harvesting hay. It's something you will always remember. The ranchers are out tending to their daily chores. They struggle to make a living, love what they do, and appreciate where they live. These people are proud of their heritage. From past generations to the young people of today they have built the stability of the rural West. Meeting all these wonderful folks always brings me pleasure and the excitement of another story and photo opportunity. Join me on another adventure as I share with you, *Cowboys, Cowgirls & Wide Open Spaces*, and their lives.

Opposite: Ranching families stay togethe play together and pray togethe

Anyone loose a sho

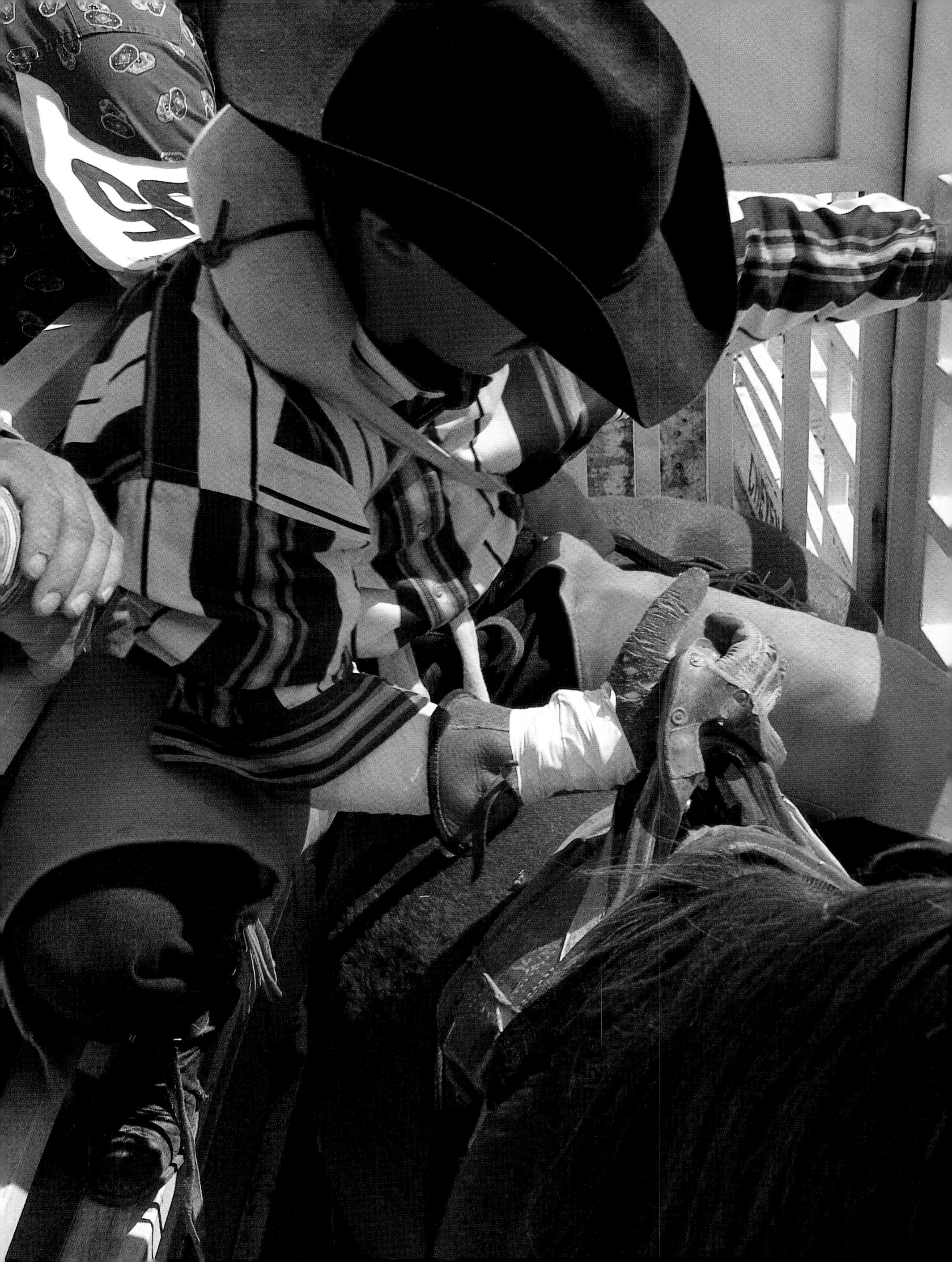

CHEYENNE FRONTIER DAYS

Billed as the "Grandaddy of Them All," and it is.
Come, see, and enjoy for yourself.
It attracts tens of thousands of people every year.
There are the rides, the grand midway, merchant booths,
lots of food, night time music and entertainment.
But most of all it's cowboys, bucking horses and excitement.

Cheyenne Frontier days attracts everyone.

A cowboy always has a guitar and sings to a lady.

DAYS

BELL RANCH
M HACIENDA
9 M MULE CAMP
HEADQUARTERS 19 M
WEST CAMP 10 M
LA CINTA 4 M
COLORADO 1 M

BELL RANCH, NEW MEXICO

The beautiful Bell Ranch is located in northeastern New Mexico. The title dates back to 1824 as the Pablo Montoya Grant. By the 1900's the ranch was 719,000 acres, with about 22,000 head of cattle and 1,000 horses. At present the ranch is 292,000 acres. That's a brief history, but the real story is how well the ranch is doing today.

I stopped by one sunny afternoon and talked to Rusty Tinnin, ranch manager, as to when I could get some cowboy shots. He said there would be a calf branding in a few days. If I could be here at 6 AM I would have a full day of photographing.

After driving about 45 minutes at sunrise on their wide open range I found the branding location. It was a wonderful opportunity to photograph them, with about 170 calves to do. First order of the day was rounding up that section of the pasture and cutting the dry cows from the rest of the herd. The cowboys were out before sunrise to get the herd together and move them to the branding pens. The bulls were put into a separate pen.

The littlest cowboy

The crew was super and totally supportive of my photography presence. “Now Jon remember, the horses have the right of way so watch your toes!” A quote of wisdom from one of the cowboys to watch where I go around the branding. Quick on your feet is the rule of the day. They have the ropers that lasso the back feet of the calves, then they are dragged to be branded. The calves showed no discomfort from the ordeal and trotted back to the rest of the herd when they were finished.

Some of the cowboys brought their children to work the branding. It was a great education for the kids. They worked as hard as the rest of the adults. Weather was excellent and I shot lots of film. At the finish they invited me for a cowboy’s lunch on the range. Was it ever grand. At 1 pm I was heading north to Colorado.

Visit a town that was too tough to die. This is Buckskin Joe. The buildings have been moved from various parts of the West and are totally authentic. Located West of Canon City, Colorado and right next to the Royal Gorge. You will have an exciting time. The grand old days of the West will not let you down. Each day there are gun fights taken from the pages of history and comedy skits to entertain the visitors. Over the years many movie and TV shows have been filmed here including: *Conagher, The Sacketts,* and *How The West Was Won.* I have enjoyed visiting them and photographing their shows. You will leave with wonderful memories.

BUCKSKIN JOE FRONTIER TOWN & RAILROAD

GLENN WILLIAMS

Glen was born on the great wide open plains of western Texas. I met him and his wife one summer day in the Colorado high country. Glen makes custom saddles and because of their popularity he can't keep them in supply. When you order one, plan on a long wait. I'm not an expert on saddles but what I saw was very impressive.

Now for a unique story. Glen's great grand-dad rode with the Chisholm family that blazed the famous trail. Following that he went to New Mexico with John Chisholm to start a cattle business and he rode with Billy the Kid. I thought that was an interesting bit of family history.

THE TEXAS COWBOYS' CHRISTMAS BALL

Stepping back into another time in Anson, Texas is what the *Texas Cowboys' Christmas Ball* is all about. The year is 1885 and the town of Anson is made up of dirt streets, dusty roads and the Star Hotel. Local hotel operator, M. G. Rhodes decided to do something special for all the cowboys in the area. So he gathered the people from far and wide for a special time to celebrate. The rules were simple: No guns, spurs or hats allowed, and the ladies had to wear dresses. The gals came from all around, dressed to kill in their splendid style. Their long flowing dresses graced the dance floor.

One hundred and fifteen years later the ball is still going strong and growing every year. The only difference is that the cowboys drive to the ball in their pickup trucks and SUV's instead of riding their horses. Inside Pioneer Hall, decorations cover the walls and the stage is glittered with dazzling color. The cowboys check their hats at the coat room and ladies check their hair in the mirror. Being a family affair, the kids may have more fun than the adults. Scooting all about, they certainly do their share on the dance floor. Cold soda and eats are available to wet your whistle and give some extra energy.

Bernie and Suanne Holtman serve as coordinators and hosts for the annual event. The association consists of 18 members. The only income that is received to keep Pioneer Hall operating is the monies taken in at the annual ball. I enjoyed hearing them share with me what the Christmas Ball is all about.

"It has been going on for so long and people are hungry for the tradition we project. It's different than anything else people have witnessed. There are no real answers why it is as it is. It's not a bar or night club setting. It's a family event. We have preserved the early folk dancing from the 1880's—polkas, shodish, waltz, two step, and the Virginia Reel. It's not just a dance it's a reenactment of the 1885 event. It's a time and social event where people get together and renew old acquaintances and friendships. People in the old days came by horse and buggy. Then they started coming in model A's and now they come in their motor homes, Suburbans and trucks. It's hard to explain to anyone what it's like. People come from all over the U.S. We've even had calls from Australia, and kids here from Russia. All I know it's kind of magical and people enjoy it." Bernie.

"This past year, December 2000, was the 66th reenactment of the original Cowboy Christmas Ball. In addition to having a Christmas Ball, the owner of the Star Hotel gave the newly weds throughout this area a grand ball. We honor those newly wedded couples here today. Association members have to dress in period clothes. Every night it's just like the poem says, 'A livelygated Sworray' where once again we slip back in time when life was a little slower and our etiquette was a little more respected." Suanne.

As the sun drops slowly in the West and the golden-red rays cast beautiful fleeting shadows you arrive at Pioneer hall. When you step out of your car there is the wonder of magic in the cold evening air. Stars are starting to twinkle to the East. Warm and smiling people are there to greet you at the door. Check your hat and enter into a very special place where friends and family gather from miles around.

So when you travel down that road with Anson just in sight
The sun is sinking to the West on such a clear, cold night
The lights of town do twinkle as do the stars above
Then drive on up and park your car the hall is filled with love
We're waiting with the music, there is punch and cake for all
Greet your friends and dance again, ...to
The Texas Cowboys' Christmas Ball.

Opposite page: A twelve year old Lakota is active with her 4-H club and wins many ribbo
Following pages: In the heartland of Wyom
wheat fields roll as far as the eye can s

SOMBRERO RANCHES

Their offices are located in Boulder, CO., but the horses are found all over. They are leased out during the summer and returned in late fall for winter grazing. So each December and May the horses are sent on a two-day, sixty-mile trek from the home ranch in Craig to and from their feeding grounds. This was all coordinated with Keith Hagler, an all-time cowboy. A big 'Thank you' for your help, Keith.

Cowboys and cowgirls come from all over for the roundup. Lots and lots of wranglers are needed to move between five and seven hundred horses. Hooting and hollering, cracking bull whips, the crew moved the horses with precision. However, many of the horses would stop to eat grass along the way. With gentle persuasion off they would go again. Photographing in the midst of such a huge herd of horses was both challenging and exciting, definitely a very memorable event.

Independence Rock along the Oregon Trail in Wyoming. One of the first wagon trains through stopped here at 4th of July. There must be a thousand names carved in the rock. Climb it yourself. It's steep but very do-able.

There are certain people that you meet along life's way who make a wonderful impression on you and you will never forget them.

BAXTER BLACK

Well now how can I get Baxter to be a part of my cowboy book? I just call him. I must say, Baxter was accommodating and a wonderful person to chat with. Let me share with you a little history of Baxter Black. Baxter grew up in Las Cruces, NM. He was busy in school and got involved in riding bulls and studying agriculture. His comment is: "You either are or are not a cowboy." While in college he decided to become a veterinarian. "So how did you become a poet?" I asked him. "Well, when I would be out tending the ranchers' cattle, horses, or whatever, I would spend several days working on one ranch. At night I would hear stories about what their everyday life was like. I started to put these stories together in poetry form. As I would go to other ranches I would share the stories and turn it into poetry and it just took off from there. Actually I thought I was a song writer but I was a long way from Nashville."

Baxter has been on television, radio, and live stage where he shares his poetry with people face to face. He is acclaimed as the number one selling cowboy poet. He is a columnist and radio commentator and has several books on his poetry, along with audio and video tapes. Baxter has three objective he strives for in his poetry:

1. Perfect meter and rhyme
2. Original thought
3. A strong ending.

After hearing his poetry and humor and reading one of his books, it is obvious Baxter definitely loves his work and loves people. When he is in your area be sure to see him.

On a warm spring day, ranches of the majestic Arkansas River Valley. Mt. Princeton in the background.

BRADY, TEXAS

I was fortunate to catch Gray Carrithers at his ranch in the beautiful Hill Country. It was spring and the blue bonnets were everywhere. Gray's great grandfather bought 4,259 acres in 1896 and by 1963 it had increased to 23,580 acres. The Staten Creek Ranch is now in its fourth generation of operation. I sat with Gray and his wife, Marilyn, in a beautiful rock house located along the San Saba River.

The original two room homestead is still standing out back. The walls are eighteen inches thick and it stays nice and cool inside during the long hot summers. "We didn't have electricity till 1967." Gray shared with me. "At one time we ran about 2500 head of cattle. Back in the old days we never had any trouble from the Indians but there was always cattle rustling going on. Once the river flooded and came right up to where we are now sitting. As for the cattle operation, we have Brahman bulls and cross them with Hereford cows. That makes F1 heifers and they sell well on the market. We also have Angus bulls and cross them with herefords which produces the black white face you saw driving in."

It took me about 35 minutes driving off the highway to reach his home. The oak, mesquite trees and rolling hills are hiding all kinds of back country treasures. In fact, it is told that Jim Bowie hid a lot of silver in the area on his way to the Alamo. Since then people have found old pistols, a Bowie knife and other items.

This is Bettye. A genuine Texan. Cheers!

Only in Texas will you find striped horses.

NATIONAL RANCHING HERITAGE CENTER

Located in Lubbock, Texas it is a testimony to the life of the ranchers and pioneers of the West. You will find a fascinating museum center with ranching history of the early West. Outside there are 35 or more authentic ranch buildings brought into the historical park. This was a dream of Dr. Grover Murray, then President of Texas Tech University. With hard work and much planning, the formal opening was July 2, 1976. In the year 2001, they are celebrating their twenty fifth anniversary. Today more than 70,000 people visit the center, where they can view exhibits, take tours, and learn more about the Western cultural events. There are educational programs to share with children and adults alike. What I like is the warm and enthusiastic people who volunteer their time to share what the Center is all about. The stories they can share with you are magical reflections of the past. Marsha Gustafson is a wonderful host and I thank her for her time with me.

There is a storm brewing over the eastern plains. Black clouds billow high into the sky. Wind and rain come roaring through like a mighty freight train. Lightning is awesome.

A RANCHER'S LIFE

"Whoever made up the cliche, 'Blood, Sweat and Tears'...musta been a cowboy. It's up long before dawn and going hard all day long. We are servants of the land and livestock and our frosting on the cake is the knowledge that we are keeping a piece of heritage that brought this country into being.

Four-wheelers and cell phones or two-way radios are a blessing when it comes to fixing a fence or finding someone around the ranch, but horses are still the heart of getting our cattle work done. We are constantly trying to second guess several brains at once...the horse, the cows and those riding to keep this all together. We don't know what a normal work week is. That is probably the stressful part of this life. Besides guessing the weather for the day, which is a battle rarely won, you have to have faith in your horses, family, friends and God. This past year there was a bad drought and we had to work around that, too. We also have to feed with a team of horses in the winter. No matter how cold it is, they ALWAYS start!

Punching cows for a living is not financially friendly, but payday is subsidized in every sunrise, sunset, a breath of fresh air, wild critters, a new-born calf and a smiling face. Do something else with my life? Not as long as I'm breathing." Suzie Hoiness, Montana.

HUGH O'BRIAN

In junior high and high school I couldn't wait to watch Wyatt Earp on television. Wyatt was my real life western hero. The actor was Hugh O'Brian. As plans for this book evolved, I made contact with Hugh and his comment was "Jon I hope you have Wyatt Earp in it!" With that we discussed our traveling schedules and we met in Buffalo, WY.

Hugh is not one to rest on his movie successes. In 1958 he traveled to Africa for a wonderful opportunity to meet Dr. Albert Schweitzer. It became a life altering experience for him. Dr. Schweitzer was helping others, out in the middle of nowhere. Hugh decided he wanted to do something to help others, also.

That same year Hugh started a program to help high school 10th graders realize their full potential in life. It's called Hugh O'Brian Youth Leadership (HOBY for short). There are over 300,000 alumni and more than 14,500 high schools that annually participate in his program. Dr. Schweitzer remarked to Hugh "The most important thing in education is to teach young people to think for themselves." At HOBY the students are encouraged to set goals, learn more about business and the free enterprise system.

During the Leadership Seminars held throughout the USA, each spring, a boy and girl are selected to represent that area at the HOBY's eight day World Leadership Congress. There are also 38 to 45 other countries sending their peers to participate. The guidance and leadership is all done by adult volunteers. The response from HOBY Alumni has been overwhelming. The progress and influence they have made has been a major stepping stone in the growth of America.

Thank you, Hugh for helping to make America a better place.

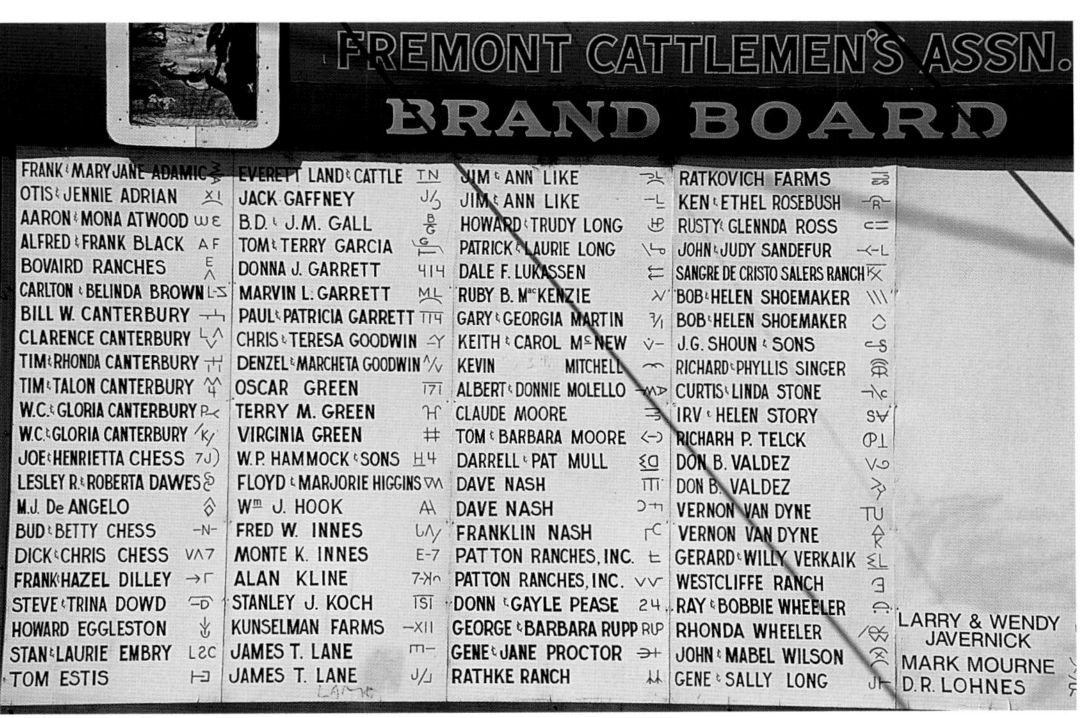

WYOMING HORSES

Found outside Pavillion is mile after mile of open range land. Off in the distance are the majestic Owl Creek Mountains. In the middle of this is Wyoming Horses Ranch. For over thirty years Lonnie and Grace Mantle have been in the horse leasing business. Now they are semiretired and have turned the operation over to their daughter and her husband, Dar and Bob Vogel. The whole family and all the wranglers are wonderful people and they really know their business. They have over one thousand horses for trail riding, stables, dude ranches, pack outfitters and those who just want to rent a horse for awhile. I was privileged to be there for their fall horse gathering. All the crew were perfect in running the horses for photography purposes. Expecting clear, vibrant blue skies and warm sunny days, it snowed. So I got my winter shots in early. Oh yes, the Sunday dinner at the ranch was more than well worth the trip.

Previous page: "Yaaaahooooo! Move those horses!"

Above: Cowboy John got new duds. His old ones just wore out.
Following page: Cowboys and fall colors in the high country.
Mt. Sopris and the mountains of Aspen in the background.

PEGGY

To the locals in a very small Colorado community, Peggy is known as "The Jill of All Trades." Having a dream of owning a horse ranch, one day she happened upon a beautiful piece of rough, raw mountain land. After purchasing it, a horse barn including a small apartment was quickly constructed because soon it would be fall. Fall in the high country is made up of sunny days but very cold nights. She ran fence lines, built horse shelters, plowed and drilled for the many needed things necessary on a ranch. Most of this she did by herself.

For the first two months she lived on a dirt floor, had no heat or running water other than the artesian spring that runs constantly on her property. There were long, physically draining days. She was up long before dawn and finally resting sometime after dark. By November the dirt floor was cemented and tiled. The room was warmed by a wood burning stove. In December she celebrated the arrival of indoor plumbing. But at night she slept under a pile of blankets topped by a sleeping bag to stay warm. Many mornings she was greeted with frost on the inside walls.

But Peggy struggled through. A late spring blizzard stormed her in for three days in May, during which a baby colt was born, coincidentally on her birthday. He is appropriately named Stormy. At last count she has nine horses along with some dogs, cats, goats and ducks. Four of her horses are adopted from Rescue Foundations, something else she had dreamed of doing. When she is out and about, the horses whinny at her presence and follow her around in their pastures. Through all of this, she successfully telecomutes to her regular job. Good news though, her log home is now finished and she stays warm and cozy inside.

"This afternoon I was playing with the dog in the barn, had the Lonesome Dove music playing, was watching two horses romping in the arena together, looked out at the incredible views, and the tears just started streaming down my face. But they were very happy tears. It finally hit me, I've accomplished a dream." Peggy.

As the sun slowly rises in the East it shines its early morning purple magic on the snow covered mountains to the south. Birds sing their music in the cool dawn air. The deer quietly eat field grass next to her home. It's quiet and still outside. With a smile on her face and love in her heart, this is the Peggy who can do all things.

REGISTERED
TEXAS
LONGHORNS

BLACK MOUNTAIN RANCH

Located in the heart of the Colorado Rocky Mountains, secluded among aspens, one-in-a-million views, and spectacular wildlife this beautiful guest ranch draws people to it. Nowell and Tootie May have been running their dream ranch for nine years. It's now becoming "The" place to be. They have worked hard and long hours to make it into a first class guest ranch destination. Hop on one of their many friendly horses and take an exciting trail ride with their seasoned and story telling wranglers. You will ride through aspen groves and pine trees high in the back country surrounded by mountains as far as the eye can see. Or, join a group as they herd cattle through untamed mountainous terrain. From personal observations, the cattle are trained to go in all directions which gets the riders going in all directions. Let an expert trout guide show you how to catch that elusive fish. In the summer you can also do overnight pack trips, trap shooting or cool off with some whitewater rafting. I try to make it for dinner as their fabulous dinner ride cook outs are not to be missed. After a wonderful meal and music around the camp fire, or in the log saloon, you can watch the golden rays of the setting sun cast fleeting shadows of red and purple across the endless sky. Truly breath taking! In the fall, hunt for trophy elk or deer are the activities "du jour." And in the winter you can snowmobile to your hearts content, enjoy sunset sleigh rides, or take the shuttle to nearby ski resorts for a day of downhill skiing. I drove to the ranch a total of eighteen times for a shot I needed. And it worked: it's the front cover of this book. Tootie and Nowell have followed their dream. And I like to see dreams come true.

Following pages: I photographed these wild horses in Wyoming and then spent about an hour seeing how close I could get. I ended up about 60 feet from them, ran out of time and had to leave. They never bolted.

HARRY CAREY, JR.

It was sometime in 1948 and I was in the first grade in school. I always looked in the Sunday paper for new movies coming to town. In the movie section was a full color, half page ad, *She Wore a Yellow Ribbon*. John Wayne was one of my movie cowboy heroes and I couldn't wait till the movie came to the local theater. As I watched the movie there was an actor by the name of Harry Carey, Jr. He didn't have the lead but I knew that someday I would have the opportunity to meet him. Fifty years later I did.

Harry was born into the movie business. His father, Harry Sr., made his first silent western movie in 1909. "Dobe" stepped into his father's boots as a member of the John Ford Stock Co. Oh, as for the nickname "Dobe," his dad gave him that due to his reddish/blond hair, referring to the adobe mud that is found throughout the West. Dobe now has more than 100 films to his credit including: *3 Godfathers, She Wore a Yellow Ribbon, Wagonmaster, The Searchers, Cheyenne Autumn,* and more recently *Tombstone.*

I asked Dobe what his favorite film was. "I did my best acting in in *The Searchers* but I enjoyed *3 Godfathers* best." "When you worked with John Ford you NEVER, EVER made any comments or suggestions on how to do a scene. Ol' John would absolutely go through the roof; 'Oh! So now you want to be a director do you?' Well Dobe has had a most wonderful life. He and his beautiful wife Marilyn have been married for fifty-seven years. When she was asked what was the secret to a long marriage, Marilyn replied, "A good sense of humor!" The many stories he has shared with me about working with John Wayne, Ward Bond, Ben Johnson, Maureen O'Hara, Henry Fonda and others are a once in a life time delight. Harry Jr. has made a positive impact in the history of film making. I have thoroughly enjoyed his book about his life and the movies, *Company of Heroes*.

Dobe, have a wonderful day, always.

Opposite page: The cowboy preacher travels the trails, sharing the "Word" and giving a helping hand wherever needed.

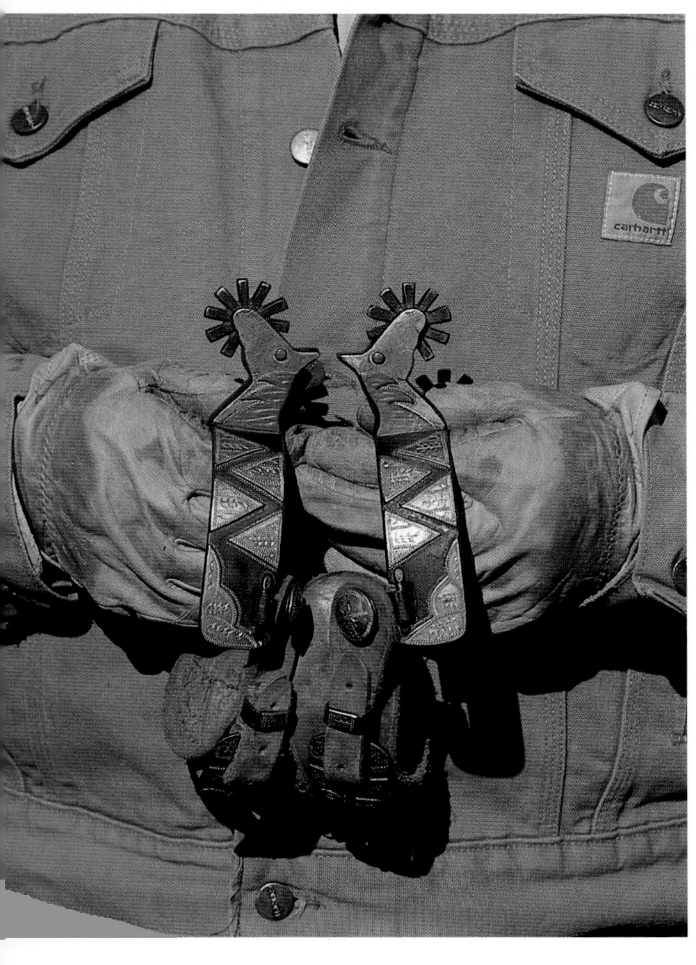

Above and following page: The Great Divide Basin in Wyoming is one of the most desolate places in America. There is absolutely nothing there except space. In some areas you will find wild horses. Oh yes! You will find antelope and they might even pose for you. Travel with caution because nobody will be by, except maybe in a few days or a week. And you don't want to be out there when it rains.

Cowboy & Cowgirl taking a well deserved break.

Opposite page: This is a Castle ghost town in the hills of Montana. Well preserved after many years of neglect. Mike, Terry and I found it on a pretty spring day.

938

PADLOCK RANCH

Found on the Wyoming and Montana state line is a rather large layout of rolling hills, open valleys and flower covered mountain sides. Dan Scott has had the ranch in his family for quite some time and much of it goes far into Montana. Their market is beef and they have a lot of it. About fifty-five employees keep the ranch going and they sell around 12,000 calves a year. Dan was delighted to have me come by and do some photography of the wranglers doing their cowboy thing. First order of the day was a 6AM yearling round up to ship off for a rodeo event. So at 6AM I was still getting the sleep out of my eyes as eight high spirited cowboys cut yearlings for the road trip of the day. Dust, dust, lots of dust and then there was a clearing. The livestock inspector was there to check the yearlings for any communicable diseases and make sure they are all Padlock Ranch animals. He was kind enough to show me the Wyoming directory for brands. Most fascinating.

There was no problem with the critters so the cattle truck rolled down the road by 9 AM. The wranglers paused long enough for a 'family' photo and then loaded their horses on various trailers. They headed off for more work elsewhere on the ranch. Ranch wife Suzie Hoiness filled me in on what goes into a typical day, summer and winter.

The time was October for the cattle drive down from the Bighorn mountains. Looking for fall colors we ended up in a major snowstorm. The cowboys spent two days getting the cattle out. I just made it out by the back roads and highway. I returned in late May during spring branding. The crew was happy to see me again and encouraged me to come and help with the branding. It was a most tempting offer but my photo agenda had me other places early that morning. After a rather hardy breakfast the cowboys were gone by three AM. By six AM they found their cattle and started their work. I slept in. About ten thirty in the morning Suzie started preparing their afternoon meal. The cowboys came back about two, and averaged about three large cuts of steak apiece plus all the other food stuffs. What a meal. Unfortunately for me it was off on another assignment and I couldn't join them.

Lamont pop 3. Yes it's pretty quiet around here, except for the wind.

Opposite: A little girl meets a cowboy.

OL' PETE

Born on the banks of a slow moving stream in Eastern Nebraska, Ol' Pete grew up riding wild horses and chasing cows all over the west. There wasn't any bucking wild horse he couldn't ride or a cow he couldn't rope. He could shoot the head off a rattle snake at the drop of a hat. Distance was never a problem. If he saw the snake it was history. With people there was a warm and gentle smile on his face. A firm hand shake and his word was his bond. When someone needed help or was in trouble Ol' Pete would always be there to help. He never took a bow or said a word of how he gave for others. His only non cowboy stint was during WWII. He enlisted in the Coast Guard and was stationed in Alaska. He loved the great wilderness that was all around him but he missed the ranch life, the wide open range, and the wind in his face off the back of a horse. Carpenter, plumber, mechanic, Ol' Pete could do it all. I am proud to call him, "My friend." When it came time, he was brought to his Father's kingdom high above the sky.

One evening I walked through the sage as a puff of wind blew across the valley. And just for a moment, in that cool gentle breeze, I could just barely hear the faint sound of bagpipes playing *Amazing Grace*. I knew Pete was home.

Sittin' on his painted horse in
the blazing setting sun
Ol' Pete toiled hard throughout
the day and now his
work was done
He rested by the evening fire
as the day turned into night
And as the stars twinkled
in the sky...he knew
his life was right.

September 11, 1916
to
April 11, 2000